ANIMALS
That Make a Difference!

Sea Otters

Ashley Lee

Explore other books at:
WWW.ENGAGEBOOKS.COM

VANCOUVER, B.C.

WWW.ENGAGEBOOKS.COM

Sea Otters: Level 3
Animals That Make a Difference!
Lee, Ashley, 1995
Text © 2023 Engage Books
Design © 2023 Engage Books

Edited by: A.R. Roumanis and Ashley Lee
Design by: Mandy Christiansen

Text set in Arial Regular.
Chapter headings set in Nathaniel-19.

FIRST EDITION / FIRST PRINTING

Page 19 bottom picture courtesy: National Science Foundation. Every reasonable effort has
been made to contact the copyright holders of all material reproduced in this book.

LIBRARY AND ARCHIVES CANADA CATALOGUING IN PUBLICATION

Title: Sea otters / Kit Caudron-Robinson.
Names: Caudron-Robinson, Kit, author.
Description: Series statement: Animals that make a difference

Identifiers: Canadiana (print) 20240387082 | Canadiana (ebook) 20240387090
ISBN 978-1-77878-617-4 (hardcover)
ISBN 978-1-77878-618-1 (softcover)
ISBN 978-1-77878-619-8 (epub)
ISBN 978-1-77878-620-4 (pdf)

Subjects:
LCSH: Sea otter—Juvenile literature.

Classification: LCC QL737.C25 C38 2024 | DDC J599.769/5—DC233

This project has been made possible in part
by the Government of Canada.

Canada

Contents

What Are Sea Otters?

Sea otters are **mammals**. They are the smallest mammals in North America. Sea otters are known for their playful behavior and strong swimming skills.

KEY WORD

Mammals: animals with warm blood and a backbone.

Sea Otters have the thickest fur of any mammal. Water cannot pass through it when it is kept clean. This helps keep them warm in cold water.

Sea otters trap air bubbles in their fur to help them float better.

A Closer Look

Sea otters are about 4 feet (1.2 meters) long. They weigh between 35 pounds (16 kilograms) and 100 pounds (45 kg).

Sea otters have webbed feet that help them swim.

A sea otter's ears will close when they go underwater.

Sea otters have pockets of skin under their arms that they store food in.

Where Do Sea Otters Live?

Sea otters often live near rocky beaches or kelp forests on ocean **coasts**. They do not live in caves, nests, or dens. They often sleep in the open water while floating on their backs.

KEY WORD

Coasts: areas where the land meets the ocean.

Russian sea otters live near Russia and Japan. Southern sea otters can be found near California. Northern sea otters live in the Pacific Ocean between Alaska and Washington.

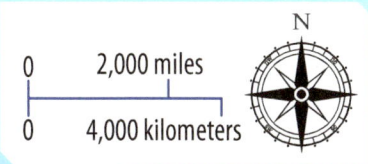

Alaska and Washinton

Russia

Canada

China

Japan

Pacific Ocean

United States

California

Russia and Japan

Australia

0 ⊢——⊣ 2,000 miles

0 ⊢——⊣ 4,000 kilometers

N

Legend
▪ Land
▫ Ocean

9

What Do Sea Otters Eat?

Sea otters mostly eat shellfish. Shellfish are animals that live in water and have shells. Crabs, clams, mussels, and sea urchins are all kinds of shellfish that otters eat.

Sea otters sometimes dive 250 feet (76 meters) underwater to find food.

Sea otters use rocks to crack open shells. They eat their food while floating on their backs. This lets them use their chest like a table.

How Do Sea Otters Talk to Each Other?

Sea otters make many different sounds to talk with each other. They squeak, whistle, whine, hiss, and growl. Baby sea otters called pups squeak to talk to their moms. They will cry if they are away from their mothers for too long.

Sea otters may make a cooing sound when they are around another otter they like. They may whine if they are upset. They will sometimes hiss if they are angry or afraid.

Sea Otter Life Cycle

Mother sea otters usually only have one pup at a time. Pups are often born in the water with their eyes open. New pups cannot swim, but they do float on the surface of the water.

Sea otters start to swim at about four weeks old. They cannot dive underwater until they are about six weeks old. Until then, a mother sea otter will wrap kelp around her pup to keep it from floating away while she dives for food.

A sea otter will stay with its mother until the mother is ready to have another pup. This happens six months to a year after birth. A sea otter cannot have its own pup until it is between three and five years old.

Male sea otters live for about 10 to 15 years. Female sea otters often live longer. They live for about 15 to 20 years.

Curious Facts About Sea Otters

Sea otters are one of the only mammals that use tools.

Sea otters keep their favorite shell-cracking rocks in one of their food pockets.

Sea otters can hold their breath for more than five minutes.

Sea otters spend about five hours cleaning their fur every day.

Sea otters can swim 5.6 miles (9 kilometers) per hour underwater.

Sea otters rest together in groups called rafts. They will often link arms while sleeping.

Where Did Sea Otters Come From?

Scientists think sea otters **evolved** sometime between five and seven million years ago. They believe that sea otters first appeared in Europe and Asia. Sea otters made their way to North America over time.

Some scientists think sea otters come from a weasel-like relative that lived on land. They think their bodies slowly changed over time. One change was that they lost some of their sense of smell.

KEY WORD

Evolved: changed slowly over time from something else.

19

How Sea Otters Help Earth

Sea otters eat a lot of sea urchins. This helps keep the number of sea urchins down. If there are too many sea urchins, they will eat all the kelp in an area until there is none left.

Saving kelp also helps save all of Earth. Kelp soaks up carbon dioxide. Carbon dioxide is a gas that makes **climate change** worse. Without kelp, there would be more carbon dioxide in the air.

KEY WORD

Climate change: a change in the average temperature on Earth over a long period of time.

How Sea Otters Help Other Animals

Sea otters help other animals by eating sea urchins and letting kelp grow. Many other animals need kelp for food and **shelter**. If kelp goes away, so do these other animals.

KEY WORD

Shelter: something that covers or protects someone or something.

Saving kelp does not just help animals that eat kelp. Many larger sea creatures eat the animals that eat kelp. Sea otters help keep entire **ecosystems** healthy just by eating one of their favorite foods.

KEY WORD

Ecosystems: communities of living and nonliving things that work together to stay healthy.

How Sea Otters Help Humans

Many people travel to coasts to see sea otters. This helps bring in money for businesses in these areas. This money helps families live healthy and happy lives.

Sea otters help bring in about 50 million dollars to British Columbia, Canada, every year.

Otters help humans when they help Earth. Climate change can affect people's health and make them sick. It can also make it harder for people to grow food. When kelp takes carbon dioxide out of the air, it helps humans live healthier lives.

Sea Otters in Danger

Sea otters are in danger of becoming extinct. This means they may disappear forever. The biggest danger sea otters face is oil spills. Oil can get into a sea otter's fur and allow cold water to get through. They can die if they get too cold.

Sea otters almost became extinct in the 1700s and 1800s because of hunters.

Pollution from chemicals or garbage can harm sea otters. Sea otters sometimes think this garbage is food and try to eat it. This can make them sick. They can also get stuck in pieces of garbage like bags or nets.

How to Help Sea Otters

Help clean garbage off beaches in your area. This will stop it from getting into the water. Get your friends and family to join you.

Chemicals in cleaning products can end up in the ocean where they harm sea otters. Ask the adults in your house if you can switch to using nontoxic cleaning products. These are cleaning products that have been made without harmful chemicals.

Stay away from any otters you see at the beach. They are cute but may bite if you get too close.

Quiz

Test your knowledge of sea otters by answering the following questions. The questions are based on what you have read in this book. The answers are listed on the bottom of the next page.

1 What are sea otters known for?

2 What do sea otters use to crack open shells?

3 How many pups do mother sea otters usually have at a time?

4 Where do sea otters keep their favorite shell-cracking rocks?

5 How do sea otters help other animals?

6 What is the biggest danger sea otters face?

Explore other books in the
Animals That Make a Difference series

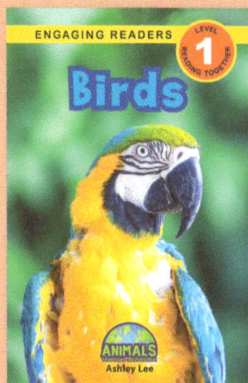

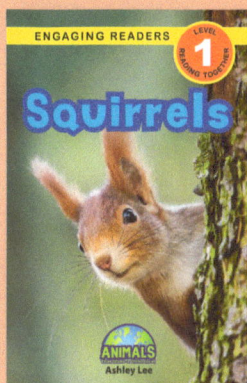

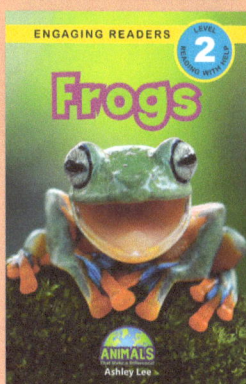

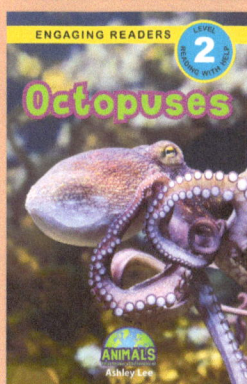

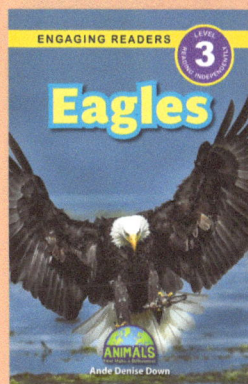

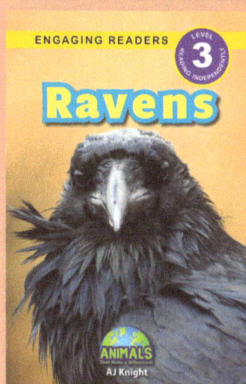

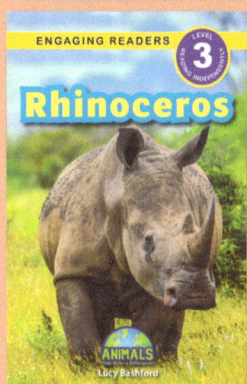

ENGAGING READERS — LEVEL 1 — **Birds** — Ashley Lee

ENGAGING READERS — LEVEL 1 — **Ladybugs** — Ashley Lee

ENGAGING READERS — LEVEL 1 — **Squirrels** — Ashley Lee

ENGAGING READERS — LEVEL 2 — **Butterflies** — Ashley Lee

ENGAGING READERS — LEVEL 2 — **Frogs** — Ashley Lee

ENGAGING READERS — LEVEL 2 — **Octopuses** — Ashley Lee

ENGAGING READERS — LEVEL 3 — **Eagles** — Ande Denise Down

ENGAGING READERS — LEVEL 3 — **Ravens** — AJ Knight

ENGAGING READERS — LEVEL 3 — **Rhinoceros** — Lucy Bashford

Visit www.engagebooks.com to explore more Engaging Readers.

6. Oil spills
5. By eating sea urchins and letting kelp grow
2. Rocks 3. One 4. In one of their food pockets
1. Their playful behavior and strong swimming skills
Answers:

Milton Keynes UK
Ingram Content Group UK Ltd.
UKHW050248081024
449408UK00007B/76